Little Devils

Story by Rebecca Johnson   *Photos by Steve Parish*

"Oh, please stop squabbling," their mother would groan.

"Why can't you be nice, quiet boys like Mrs Quoll's children?"

5

The boys would try to be good, but it never lasted.

As soon as their mother turned her back it would be on again...

wrestling, biting
and chasing,
rolling, scuffling
and growling.

7

"Stay away from those boys," Mrs Potoroo warned her son, "they are too rough."

The boys' fighting
woke Mr Wombat one morning.

"Dear me," he grumbled. "Children didn't behave like that when I was a lad."

10

One night their mother told them she had to go out the next day.
"Please be good and try not to fight," she said.

"Sure, Mum," they grinned.

But the next day
the little devils were
up even earlier.

13

They were off,
grappling and
snarling.

Suddenly,
an echidna
ran past,
puffing.

"Hide quickly," he gasped, "a feral cat is coming!" The twins stopped and looked around.

All of the other animals were in a panic, looking for somewhere to hide.

The boys weren't scared. They crept through the grass towards the cat.

Then, when they
were really close,
they jumped out
and yelled,
"RAAAH!"

The cat got such a fright, it ran away yowling. "Hooray! Hooray!" cried all the other animals.

Mrs Devil was very proud of her boys when she heard the news.

The other animals agreed that perhaps it wasn't such a bad thing for the boys to practise fighting. They were, after all, Tasmanian Devils...

23

just as long as
they didn't
start until
after 7 o'clock
in the morning.